Issues today

A resource for KS3 ...SE

Sustainability and Environment

Editor: **Lisa Firth**

ISSUE 64

Independence Educational Publishers Cambridge

First published by Independence
The Studio, High Green, Great Shelford
Cambridge CB22 5EG
England

British Library Cataloguing in Publication Data

Sustainability and environment. -- (Issues today ; v. 64)

1. Nature--Effect of human beings on--Juvenile literature. 2. Sustainability--Juvenile literature. 3. Environmental protection--Juvenile literature.

I. Series II. Firth, Lisa.

333.7'2-dc23

ISBN-13: 978 1 86168 622 0

Acknowledgements

The publisher is grateful for permission to reproduce the following material.

While every care has been taken to trace and acknowledge copyright, the publisher tenders its apology for any accidental infringement or where copyright has proved untraceable. The publisher would be pleased to come to a suitable arrangement in any such case with the rightful owner.

Chapter One: Sustainable Resources

The Environment, © The World Bank, *Sustainability and the city,* © SEPA, *Resources and consumption,* © Friends of the Earth Europe, *Waste and recycling: a quick guide,* © Crown copyright is reproduced with the permission of Her Majesty's Stationery Office, *Scandal of UK's illegal e-waste trade exposed,* © Environmental Investigation Agency, *Waste and recycling,* © Crown copyright is reproduced with the permission of Her Majesty's Stationery Office.

Chapter Two: Safeguarding the Planet

A history of climate change, © Crown copyright is reproduced with the permission of Her Majesty's Stationery Office, *The marine environment,* © Crown copyright is reproduced with the permission of Her Majesty's Stationery Office, *Flood and droughts,* © Global Water Partnership, *Population and the environment,* © Population Action International, *Water statistics,* © WaterAid, *Forgotten forests have vital role in keeping deserts at bay,* © CIWEM.

All illustrations, including the cover, are by Don Hatcher.

Editorial by Cara Acred and layout by Jackie Staines, on behalf of Independence Educational Publishers.

Printed in Great Britain by MWL Print Group Ltd.

Lisa Firth
Cambridge
April 2012

ISSUES today

Sustainability and Environment

Contents

Chapter One: Sustainable Resources

Chapter Two: Safeguarding the Planet

ISSUES today

A resource for KS3

About Key Stage 3

Key Stage 3 refers to the first three years of secondary schooling, normally years 7, 8 and 9, during which pupils are aged between 11 and 14.

This series is also suitable for Scottish P7, S1 and S2 students.

About *Issues Today*

Issues Today is a series of resource books on contemporary social issues for Key Stage 3 pupils. It is based on the concept behind the popular *Issues* series for 14- to 18-year-olds, also published by Independence.

Each volume contains information from a variety of sources, including government reports and statistics, newspaper and magazine articles, surveys and polls, academic research and literature from charities and lobby groups. The information has been tailored to an 11 to 14 age group; it has been rewritten and presented in a simple, straightforward format to be accessible to Key Stage 3 pupils.

In addition, each *Issues Today* title features handy tasks and assignments based on the information contained in the book, for use in class, for homework or as a revision aid.

Issues Today can be used as a learning resource in a variety of Key Stage 3 subjects, including English, Science, History, Geography, PSHE, Citizenship, Sex and Relationships Education and Religious Education.

About this book

Sustainability and Environment is the sixty-fourth volume in the *Issues Today* series.

Our everyday lives have a huge impact on the world around us. The ways in which our actions affect the environment are much debated, and there is growing concern over the amount of natural resources we consume. *Sustainability and Environment* explores global- and UK-centred topics including sustainability, climate change, waste management and the world's growing population.

Sustainability and Environment offers a useful overview of the many issues involved in this topic. However, at the end of each article is a URL for the relevant organisation's website, which can be visited by pupils who want to carry out further research.

Because the information in this book is gathered from a number of different sources, pupils should think about the origin of the text and critically evaluate the information that is presented. Does the source have a particular bias or agenda? Are you being presented with facts or opinions? Do you agree with the writer?

At the end of each chapter there are two pages of activities relating to the articles and issues raised in that chapter. The 'Brainstorm' questions can be done as a group or individually after reading the articles. This should prompt some ideas and lead on to further activities. Some suggestions for such activities are given under the headings 'Oral', 'Moral Dilemmas', 'Research', 'Written' and 'Design' that follow the 'Brainstorm' questions.

For more information about *Issues Today* and its sister series, *Issues* (for pupils aged 14 to 18), please visit the Independence website.

www.independence.co.uk

The environment

THE NATURAL WORLD is fragile, and needs care and respect from all people.

What is the environment?

Your surroundings, and how they influence your development. The environment is made up of physical, biological, social, cultural and political conditions that determine what an organism is like and how it survives.

The environment influences how people live and how societies develop. The environment can also pose risks. Air pollution, waterborne diseases, toxic chemicals and natural disasters are some of the challenges the environment presents for mankind.

Why should I care?

Each year around the world:

- Three million people die prematurely from waterborne diseases.
- About 400,000 children under five die from diarrhoea in India alone.
- Around 1.6 million people die from exposure to cooking stove smoke inside their homes. About half of these deaths occur in India and China. Most victims are children and women from poor rural families who lack access to safe water, sanitation and modern household fuels.
- One million people die from malaria, mostly in Sub-Saharan African countries.
- One million people die from urban air pollution.
- Respiratory infections, diarrhoea and malaria account for more than 20% of deaths in developing countries, according to the World Health Organization's *Burden of Disease* report.

Pollution has greater consequences:

- Fisheries are destroyed.
- Crops are damaged.
- Production costs rise for industries that must filter dirty air or water to maintain product quality.

Extreme weather events (tornadoes, floods, hurricanes) are occurring more frequently and affecting more people than ever before. Poor people are the most vulnerable to environmental hazards.

As people move to cities from the countryside in search of better jobs, environmental problems will increase, as will the burden for poor people living in slums.

The environment

DID YOU KNOW

The United Nations Millennium Development Goals are made up of eight international development goals, decided in the year 2000 to mark the new millennium. 193 United Nations member states and over 20 international organisations agreed that they will work to achieve these goals by 2015.

What is the international community doing?

Environmental sustainability is a major global concern and is one of the United Nations Millennium Development Goals.

Many organisations are searching for ways to use natural resources so they last for our lifetimes and remain available for generations to come.

Making sure that economic, social and environmental progress can all happen at the same time is difficult and often means difficult choices. Trade-offs among generations, social groups and countries influence what people see as sustainable development.

Concern for a sound global environment is an important part of the World Bank's work to fight poverty. Environmental health is especially important in this work. The World Bank lends money to countries for environmental projects. It also requires environmental safeguards when lending money for development projects.

> ***"Environmental sustainability is a major global concern and is one of the United Nations Millennium Development Goals."***

Level of thought given to loss of biodiversity in the UK, 2007, 2009 and 2011

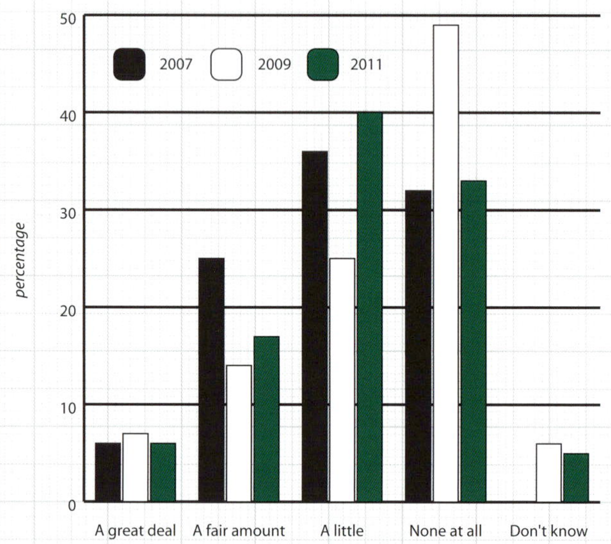

Source: Attitudes and knowledge relating to biodiversity and the natural environment, 2007-2011, *DEFRA, © Crown copyright*

Information from The World Bank. © 2011 The World Bank

www.youthink.worldbank.org

Mini glossary

determine – *decide; dictate*

organism – *living thing*

waterborne – *carried in the water*

toxic – *poisonous*

fishery – *a business that catches, processes and farms fish*

vulnerable – *weak; open to being hurt by something or someone*

environmental sustainability – *making sure that something is sustainable means using resources in a way that will not damage them or use them up completely. It is important that we think about ways to protect our environment so that it is sustainable for future generations*

environmental safeguards – *protective measures put in place to keep the environment safe from harm*

Sustainability and the city

AN EXTRACT FROM SEPAView, the magazine by the Scottish Environment Protection Agency.

We need towns and cities. Most of us live in them, most of us work in them and they are our centres of culture, education and recreation. But towns and cities have needs: for space, for energy, water and food (usually transported over many miles) and for quality shared infrastructure and services. All those needs have consequences for the environment. With 50% of the UK's carbon dioxide emissions coming from the use of buildings and the emissions from construction and transport taken into account, towns and cities make a major contribution to climate change. Is it possible, then, for cities to be sustainable, and can they play a part in combatting climate change?

Creating sustainable places

Creating sustainable places is part of how we can tackle climate change. One way to help achieve that is through the use of green infrastructure. Green infrastructure is the planned network of green spaces, like parks or green-belt land, and environmental features that help to support natural processes in an urban area. Making sure that green infrastructure is in place helps to balance out the effects of climate change, and improves the health, happiness and prosperity of local communities.

Green infrastructure can help to balance the effects of climate change by managing temperature, water resources, surface water, flooding and habitat networks. UK climate projections predict increasing summer temperatures and higher incidences of extreme weather such as heatwaves. Urban environments also experience the 'heat island' effect, where they are warmer than the surrounding countryside.

Increased temperatures in urban areas increase the impact of air pollution, which if not properly managed can lead to damaged health. Open spaces can help reduce the effects of high temperatures by allowing air to circulate and have a cooling effect. Trees, especially those with large canopies, create shade, and water evaporating from trees and plants helps to cool air temperatures. Increasing all these elements, for example by creating more parks, will help urban areas to remain comfortable places to live and work.

DID YOU KNOW?

Banff National Park in Canada built 24 wildlife crossings across the four-lane Trans-Canada Highway in order to help preserve the natural habitat of the park, increase habitat connectivity, and ensure that the road did not damage the local environment.

Sustainability and the city

Working with water

Maintaining the quantity and quality of our water supply is essential. Sealed surfaces, such as roads and pavements, stop water entering the ground, reaching aquifers and recharging groundwater. Trees, plants and green roofs provide soft ground that soaks up water and allows infiltration, and can also act as filters to remove pollutants.

Increasingly during periods of heavy rainfall, there is too much water entering the sewer system. This is because of the growing amount of sealed surfaces in towns and cities, which reduce natural drainage and increase the volume and speed of run-off. This can then lead to flooding. Surface water run-off can be reduced by introducing Sustainable Urban Drainage Systems (SUDS). SUDS mimic natural drainage, slowing and absorbing surface water. They can include green roofs, swales, wooded areas, ponds and wetlands.

The risk of flooding is increasing but the impact it has can be reduced. By working with natural processes, green infrastructure can help to manage flooding. This can include:

- The creation of vegetated land which allows water to be absorbed into the ground or taken up by plants rather than entering the river system.
- Identifying areas that can be allowed to flood naturally without causing damage, such as the creation of urban wetlands.
- Encouraging wetland plants and vegetation alongside river banks because these slow the flow of flood waters.

Green infrastructure can help maintain existing, and create new, areas of habitat, bringing biodiversity into urban areas. It also plays an important role in allowing animals to migrate. This is particularly important for species that are vulnerable to the changing climate. Wildlife corridors, which are areas of vegetation along roads, railways and rivers, can provide the connecting habitats that are needed to help species adapt to climate change.

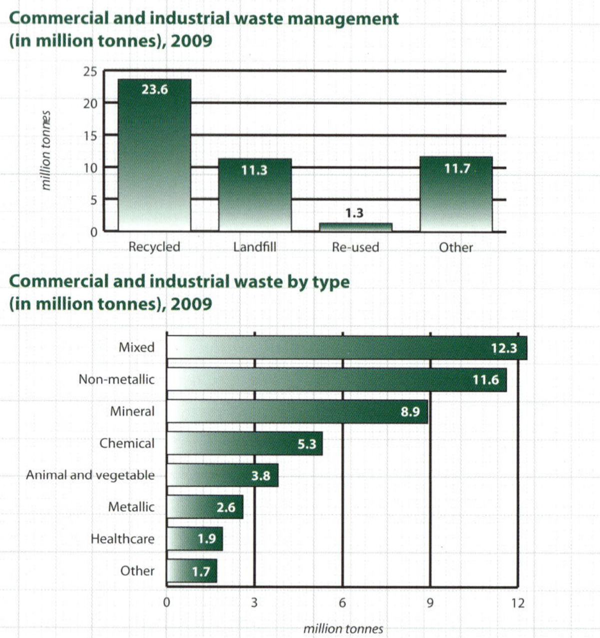

Source: Government review of waste policy in England 2011 *Department for Environment, Food and Rural Affairs, © Crown copyright*

Information from Scottish Environment Protection Agency (SEPA). © SEPA

www.sepa.org.uk

Mini glossary

recreation – *leisure*

infrastructure – *facilities and services that make it possible for a town, city, country or community to function. For example, roads, schools, power*

combating – *fighting*

green-belt land – *an area of countryside, usually around a large city, that is protected and maintained. People are not allowed to build on green belt areas*

urban – *relating to a city or town*

prosperity – *success; wealth*

aquifer – *a layer of water underground*

groundwater – *water that is held in the soil, beneath the Earth's surface*

green roof – *a roof that is covered with plants/ grass. Green roofs help to absorb rainwater*

swale – *an area of land that is moist. Can be man-made or natural.*

biodiversity – *a variety of plants and animals existing together*

Resources and consumption

RESOURCES AND CONSUMPTION campaign by Friends of the Earth Europe.

Europe is using more and more of the world's resources, and is now more dependent on imported resources than any other region.

The Earth's ability to sustain this pattern is already being pushed to the limit. But Europe's dependence on imported resources also makes it economically vulnerable, with both social and environmental impacts.

Friends of the Earth Europe is calling on the EU to take the first steps to tackle this issue by ensuring that our resource use is measured, and by adopting new policies, such as higher recycling targets.

> **Environmental problems related to European production and consumption are getting worse.**

Why is resource use important?

Natural resources are the foundation of our economy. Without the constant use of natural resources neither our economy nor our society could function. Nature provides humans with all the resources necessary for life, including:

- energy for heat, electricity and mobility;
- metals for high-tech equipment;
- wood for furniture and paper products;
- construction materials for our roads and houses;
- food and water for a healthy diet.

As global standards of living increase, and the world's population gets bigger, we are making more and more demands on the planet. This is creating competition between different regions of the world, with high prices affecting the poor, and disagreement over how we should use resources: for example, whether land is used for food, fuels or biodiversity.

Resource use: a key sustainability issue

Our consumption of natural resources includes not just physical materials but also global ecosystems and services. Climate change is the first big environmental problem that humanity is facing. However, other ecological problems include:

- the oceans being emptied of fish far faster than they can replenish themselves;
- forests being cleared for animal feed and fuel crops such as soya and oil palm;
- ecosystems and habitats increasingly being put in danger by pollution from industrial activity.

EU environmental policy – past, present and future

Over the past 30 years Europe has made a lot of progress in tackling environmental problems caused by harmful substances, such as air pollutants, sewage and hazardous waste. But environmental problems related to European production and consumption are getting worse.

It is true that the EU has improved the amount of product it can make for one euro, pound or dollar. However, this has not reduced the amount of natural resources that the EU consumes.

Current EU environmental policies fail to address the problem of rising resource use in a resource-limited world:

- Despite years of discussion, the EU still doesn't measure its resource use, new polices are not assessed to see how much difference they make, and the EU has no targets to reduce our resource use.
- Through its 'Raw Materials Initiative', the EU has shown more interest in helping developing countries have access to resources than in producing resources that are more affordable. This means that stopping poverty and helping development in these countries is put at risk.

Resources and consumption

How can we measure Europe's resource use?

The EU does not currently measure its overall use of resources, which makes it difficult to set targets or measure them.

Friends of the Earth Europe, together with the Sustainable Europe Research Institute (SERI) in Vienna, have come up with a set of effective and achievable indicators of resource use:

- Material use (this includes the materials used in making imported products).
- Total land use of countries (including via imported products), or the land used to make a product.
- Water use of a country (including via imported products), or the water footprint of a product.
- Greenhouse gas emissions (including emissions from imported products), or the carbon footprint of products.

These can be used to highlight issues that should be investigated – i.e. if a new policy results in a big increase in EU land use, then there should be further investigation.

How would the measures be used?

- The indicators can be used by the EU and governments to set targets, measure progress and create new policies (including in impact assessment of policy changes).
- They can be used by companies to assess and improve their resource use.

Next steps

Friends of the Earth Europe wants to see these resource-use indicators adopted into the EU policy-making process. By doing so Europe will be taking the first steps to becoming not just a decarbonised but also a highly resource-efficient economy, with the social, environmental and economic benefits that would bring.

"Europe is using more and more of the world's resources, and is now more dependent on imported resources than any other region."

Information from the non-governmental organisation (NGO) Friends of the Earth Europe. © Friends of the Earth Europe

www.foeeurope.org

Mini glossary

import *– something which is brought in from another country or region*

greenhouse gas emissions *– when certain harmful gases are produced (emitted) by vehicles or industrial processes, causing damage to the ozone layer. These are called 'greenhouse gases' because they cause the Earth's temperature to rise. They include Carbon Monoxide, Carbon Dioxide and Sulphur Dioxide*

impact assessment *– looking at what effect something will have, considering different criteria*

policies *– a principal or course of action, often adopted by governments and companies*

consumption *– use of something*

foundation *– the base upon which something is built and without which it could not be supported*

standard of living *– the level of comfort and affluence which people are able to enjoy*

pollutant *– any substance which has a harmful or damaging effect on the surrounding environment*

Waste and recycling: a quick guide

YOU CAN RECYCLE a wide range of rubbish, from paper and glass to batteries, televisions and clothes. This saves energy and raw materials, and reduces the amount of waste sent to landfill sites. You can also help to reduce waste at home by composting and by repairing and reusing items.

The waste hierarchy

There are many ways of disposing of waste. The waste hierarchy lists these methods from the most environmentally-friendly option to the least for many types of waste:

1. Prevention – the best option, this focuses on reducing waste being produced in the first place.
2. Reuse – for example, using old food containers as lunch boxes or old plastic bags as bin liners.
3. Recycle – taking materials from old products to make something new, like making car parts from old metal drinks cans.
4. Energy recovery – creating energy from waste, for example by burning it to produce electricity.
5. Disposal – the worst option for most types of waste as this often involves burying rubbish in landfill.

> **“Some items contain hazardous materials and need to be carefully disposed of to avoid environmental problems like water pollution.”**

Prevention – reduce waste

Recycling can help save materials and energy. It's even better to reduce the amount of things that are wasted in the first place.

The best way of doing this is simply by using less. Try asking yourself if you need a product before buying it, and taking your own bags when you go shopping.

You can also be careful about what you buy. Choose items that will last longer and try to buy products you can use again instead of disposable items.

Reuse and repair

Repairing or reusing items means that they will last longer and won't need replacing with new items so quickly.

Even when you have finished with something, someone else will often be able to use it. Second-hand furniture, clothes and electrical items like mobiles are especially popular: why not pass them on to friends and family? You could also sell them, donate them to charity or pass them on via sharing schemes.

Try looking for items you want from auction sites or giveaway sites like Freecycle or Freegle. You may even bag yourself a bargain.

> **“Around a third of all household waste collected by local authorities is organic waste which could be composted.”**

Recycle

Paper, glass, plastic bottles, garden waste, fridges, shoes, batteries – all of these and more can be recycled, helping to save energy and new materials.

Most councils run recycling collections from your doorstep, while waste and recycling centres (the local tip) can also accept many other materials for recycling.

An average family can double or even treble the amount they recycle.

Products made from recycled goods save raw materials and increase the demand for recycled materials. You can buy recycled household goods and fashion items like shoulder bags, plastic trays, pencil cases and aluminium foil.

Waste and recycling: a quick guide

Energy recovery – compost your garden and food waste

Around a third of all household waste collected by local authorities is organic waste (garden and food) which could be composted.

If organic waste is sent to landfill, it produces methane, which has strong climate change effects. Composting waste like teabags, vegetable peelings, shredded paper and egg boxes reduces these climate change effects and saves valuable space in landfill sites.

It's easy to make compost, and it provides a rich and natural source of nourishment for your garden. Many councils provide compost bins at a reduced rate, so contact your local council to find out what is available in your area.

DID YOU KNOW

Each UK household produces over 1 tonne of rubbish every year. This means that the UK creates around 31 million tonnes of rubbish annually.

Source: Green Box Day

Dispose of hazardous waste items safely

Some items contain hazardous materials and need to be carefully disposed of to avoid environmental problems like water pollution. Examples of things that need to be disposed of at a proper facility include: paint, batteries, electrical equipment and oil.

Electrical equipment and batteries can all be recycled and the precious resources used to make new items.

Information from Directgov. © Crown copyright

www.direct.gov.uk

Mini glossary

landfill sites *– places where rubbish is taken and buried after being collected from homes and businesses*

hierarchy *– a system where things are ranked in order of importance or priority*

Scandal of UK's illegal e-waste trade exposed

A TOXIC FLOOD of discarded technology is illegally leaving the UK to wash up in Africa, the Environmental Investigation Agency (EIA) reveals.

Disposing of e-waste is fast becoming big business and EIA's 18-month undercover operation shows that the chance to make a quick buck at the expense of the developing world is too tempting for some to resist.

What is e-waste?

E-waste is made up of everyday electrical goods such as mobile phones, televisions, stereos, laptops, PCs and printers. European Union regulations require it to be properly recycled, either here or in other developed countries.

But EIA investigators have uncovered a highly lucrative international e-waste black market involving many players at every level, from small businesses to large organisations, local councils and even major central government institutions.

Illegally shipped out in bulk to developing countries, e-waste is stripped down to its basic parts by primitive methods: copper wires are bundled and set alight to remove flame-resistant coatings, releasing poisonous chemicals; CRT monitors are smashed with hammers, releasing plumes of lead dust.

Poverty drives young children to carry out this work to help support their families, and the potential health consequences for them are dire – reproductive and developmental problems, damaged immune, nervous and blood systems, kidney damage and impaired brain development in the young.

The UK appears to be an especially large contributor to the problem, with the majority of its illegal shipments arriving in Nigeria and Ghana, despite appearing to work under the scrutiny of companies approved by local government.

African countries need good quality second-hand electronic goods, but the high demand for items such as TVs, PCs and fridges is being exploited by traders and 'waste tourists', Africans who travel to the UK to buy used electronic goods. Often, when their shipment arrives in African ports it is about 75 per cent waste but the profits to be made from the working goods are enough to make it worthwhile.

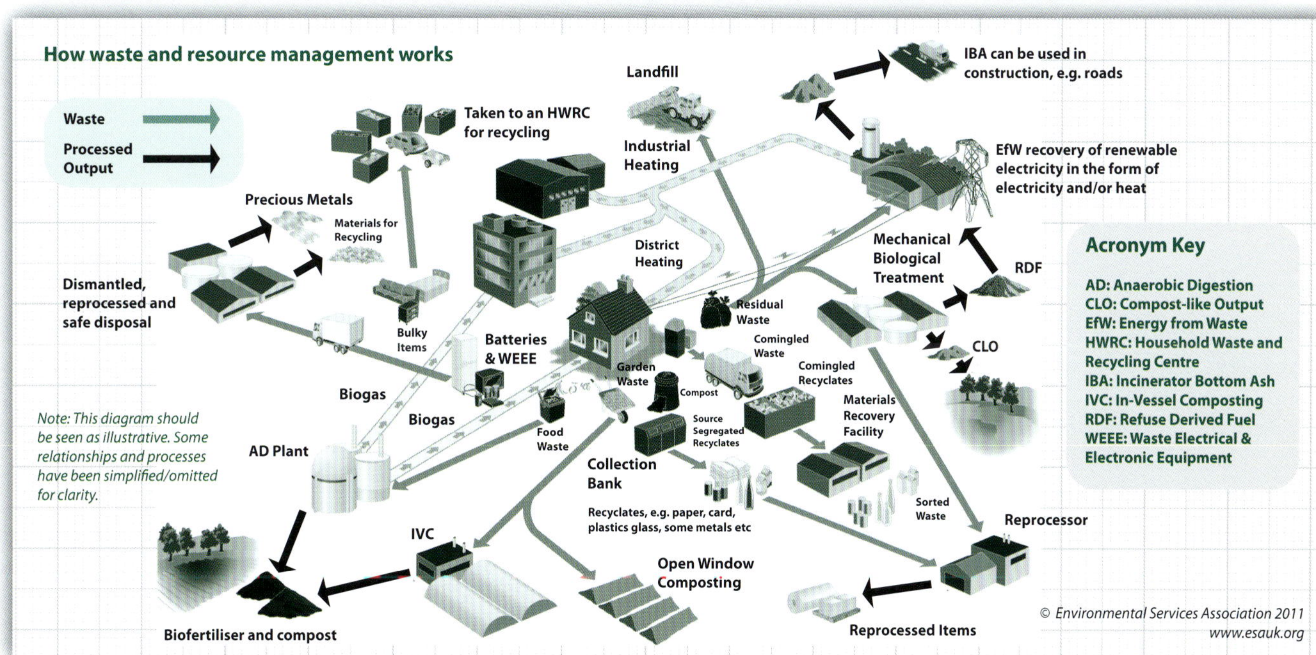

Scandal of UK's illegal e-waste trade exposed

EIA investigations

In 2009, the EIA set out to investigate smuggling networks by creating a fake company to negotiate with companies involved in exporting and trading in e-waste.

Investigators learned how traders frequently get around customs checks by mislabelling waste CRTs as working, using general terms such as 'personal effects' or 'used household goods' on shipping documents and adopting a 'no-questions-asked' approach.

EIA was offered untested CRTs by brokers who claimed to have contracts with various government institutions, including the Ministry of Defence, the Fire Service and the NHS.

In Spring 2010, undercover investigators visited six waste disposal sites (tips) in Greater London to look for signs of e-waste leakage. At council recycling centres in Croydon and Merton, they were shown how workers separated higher-quality TVs from others being dumped. Investigators were told the sets are purchased by another company, Sanak Ventures UK Ltd of London, which claims to refurbish them for export.

To check that only working TVs were being exported, EIA hid trackers inside TVs which were deliberately disabled beyond repair and left at the council sites. Several weeks later, one appeared in Nigeria and the other in Ghana, clearly showing neither had been tested prior to export.

Electronic waste collection at both sites is run by Environmental Waste Controls, one of the UK's largest waste and recycling management companies with high-profile clients including Morrisons, Tesco, Asda, Barclays, Hilton, MBNA and Prudential, the NHS and Network Rail. EIA's investigations indicate that similar practices may be the norm in almost 50 other council recycling sites run by the company, located in Blackburn, Leicester, Loughborough, north Wales, west London and Yorkshire.

EIA Senior Campaigner Fin Walravens commented:

"EIA's work clearly demonstrates the UK's failure to take its environmental responsibility seriously ... Our e-waste isn't a new problem and it isn't going away. It's time for the Government and enforcement agencies to give this issue the resources and attention it warrants."

16 May 2011

Information from the Environmental Investigation Agency.

www.eia-international.org

Mini glossary

discarded *– put aside/thrown away*

lucrative *– profitable, capable of making someone lots of money*

black market *– illegal trade of goods or services*

primitive *– not advanced/basic*

CRT monitors *– CRT stands for cathode ray tube, the component used to make computer screens before modern LCD screens. CRT monitors are sometimes referred to as 'fat' monitors because they are not of the flat-screen variety*

scrutiny *– watch carefully, with a critical eye*

exploit *– to take advantage of*

broker *– a person or company in the business of buying and selling goods*

Waste and recycling

THE UK CONSUMES natural resources at an unsustainable rate and contributes unnecessarily to climate change. Each year we generate over 80 million tonnes of waste, which causes environmental damage and costs businesses and consumers money.

The Government has published the findings of its review of waste policy, setting out its policies and a series of actions designed to help move towards a zero waste economy in England.

Key facts and figures

- Around 40% of waste from households is currently recycled, as of 2011, compared to 11% in 2000/01.
- The average residual waste per person has reduced by 76kg since 2006/07 to 275kg/person/year.
- 52% of commercial and industrial waste was recycled or reused in England in 2009, compared to 42% in 2002/03.
- 55% of municipal waste generated in the UK is sent to landfill, compared to an EU-27 average of 40%.
- According to RecycleNow, UK recycling saves more than 18 million tonnes of carbon dioxide a year – equivalent to taking five million cars off the road.
- The UK produces approximately seven million (five in England) tonnes of food waste per year and about 90 million (40-60 in England) tonnes of animal slurry and manure that could realistically be available for use by anaerobic digestion (AD) technology.
- In England this could generate at least 3-5 TWh (terrawatt hours) electricity per year by 2020 (a heat equivalent of 6-10 TWh).
- The UK water industry treats 66% of sewage sludge by AD, generating in the region of 1 TWh per year of electricity in 2010.

> **"UK recycling saves more than 18 million tonnes of carbon dioxide a year."**

- The diversion of biodegradable wastes to AD can reduce greenhouse gas emissions from landfill. For example, capturing the biogas from one tonne of food waste will save between a half and one tonne of CO_2 equivalent.
- Direct emissions from the waste management greenhouse gas inventory sector in the UK accounted for 3.2% of the UK's total estimated emissions of greenhouse gases in 2009. Of the 2008 total, 89% arises from landfill, 10% from waste-water handling and 2% from waste incineration (these figures are rounded).

Information from the Department for Environment, Food and Rural Affairs.

www.defra.gov.uk

DID YOU KNOW?

Each year the UK generates approximately 290 million tonnes of waste, which causes environmental damage and costs businesses and consumers money.

Mini glossary

municipal waste – *this includes household and commercial waste*

anaerobic digestion (AD) technology – *a process used to break down waste and create energy*

Activities

Brainstorm

Brainstorm to find out what you know about environmental sustainability.

1. Why do we need to take care of the environment?

2. What can we do to make our cities more sustainable?

Oral activities

3. Read *Waste and recycling* on pages 7 and 8. In pairs, discuss the different things you can do at home to help reuse or recycle rubbish. Do you already recycle? What else could you do? Write a bullet point list of your conclusions.

NOTES

4. Imagine that you have been asked to give a talk in assembly to encourage your school or college to be 'greener'. What changes could your school make, and what would the benefits be? Try to think of some fun and engaging ways to encourage people to get involved. Prepare a five-minute presentation using your ideas.

NOTES

Moral dilemma

5. Do you think we have a moral obligation to recycle our rubbish? What if it ends up costing us more when we try to be environmentally friendly? Discuss your thoughts with a partner or in a small group.

Activities

Research activities

6. Read *Resources and consumption* on pages 5-6. Choose one of the natural resources listed and use the Internet or your local library to research it further. Find out what we use that resource for, and whether there are any environmentally friendly alternatives available. If there aren't any alternatives, what could we do to help preserve this resource?

CONCLUSION ....

....

....

7. Research your local council's waste disposal and recycling activities. Do you think they do enough? What else could they do? Write a summary of your findings.

NOTES ....

....

....

Written activities

Complete the following activities in your exercise books or on a sheet of paper.

8. Read *Scandal of UK's illegal e-waste trade exposed* on pages 9-10. Rewrite the article in a way that would be accessible to primary school children.

9. Write a list of all the resources you use during a typical school day. Try to include every material you would use, including electricity, water, food, metals, wood and anything else. For example, you might start with the products you use to wash in the morning and the electricity and water you use in the shower. Which resources do you use the most? Are you surprised by how many you use?

Design activities

10. Choose something from home that is about to be thrown away, like an empty drinks bottle, a cereal box or an egg carton. Try and make that item into something new. For example, you could use the empty drinks bottle to plant some seeds, or the cereal box to make a pen-holder for your desk.

11. Imagine you work for a charity trying to draw attention to the way that the UK currently disposes of its e-waste. You have been asked to design a campaign flyer or leaflet that will explain what e-waste is, what should be done with it, and what is currently happening in developing countries.

A history of climate change

TACKLING CLIMATE CHANGE is one of the biggest challenges this generation faces, and the first step is to understand exactly what it is. This article explains how climate change was first detected, thc history of efforts to tackle it and the latest developments.

What is climate change?

The Earth's climate is not static. Over the billions of years of Earth's existence, it has changed many times in response to natural causes.

However, when people talk about 'climate change' today, they mean the changes in temperature over the last 100 years caused by human activity. During this time, the average temperature of the atmosphere near the Earth's surface has risen by about 0.75 degrees Celsius.

Nearly all climate scientists agree that global temperatures will rise further – by how much depends on future emissions of greenhouse gases, and other human activities.

If the temperature rise is high, the impact is likely to be extreme and it will be difficult to cope with. There are likely to be more intense and frequent extreme weather events – like heatwaves, floods and tropical storms – and sea levels will rise further.

Early discoveries about climate change

The first discoveries that helped explain recent climate change and global warming were in the 18th and 19th centuries:

- In 1753, Joseph Black discovered carbon dioxide.
- In 1827, Jean-Baptiste Fourier suggested that an atmospheric effect kept the earth warmer than it would otherwise be – he used the analogy of a greenhouse.
- In 1896, Svante August Arrhenius proposed that carbon dioxide emissions from the burning of coal would enhance the earth's greenhouse effect and lead to global warming.

The world's response to climate change

The first major international climate science conference was held in 1979. The conference called on governments 'to foresee and prevent potential man-made changes in climate'.

United Nations takes action

In 1988, the United Nations set up the Intergovernmental Panel on Climate Change (IPCC) to analyse and report on scientific findings. The IPCC warned that only strong measures to stop greenhouse gas emissions would prevent serious global warming.

Global targets for reducing emissions

In 1992, the Earth Summit took place in Rio de Janeiro. Here, the United Nations Framework Convention on Climate Change (UNFCCC) was signed by 154 nations. It agreed to prevent 'dangerous' warming from greenhouse gases and set voluntary targets for reducing emissions. The UK is one of a small number of countries which met this voluntary target.

Kyoto: legally binding cuts in emissions

In 1997, the Kyoto Protocol was agreed. Where the UNFCCC agreed voluntary targets, Kyoto was the first international treaty to set legally binding emissions cuts for industrialised nations. It was signed by 178 countries and came into force in 2005.

A history of climate change

Latest international action on climate change

In 2007, the IPCC announced that the planet has warmed about 0.75 degrees Celsius since the beginning of the 20th century. It said there is a greater than 90 per cent chance that global warming over the last 50 years is due to human activity. At the 2007 UN climate change conference in Bali, the world's nations agreed to negotiate on a deal to tackle climate change.

At the United Nations (UN) conference in Cancun 2010, the attendees agreed a global deal to tackle climate change. The key parts of this agreement were:

- An overall target limit of two degrees Celsius on temperature rise
- To include measures that developed and developing countries are taking on climate change in the UN agreement
- A system to assess how countries are living up to their promises on emissions
- The Green Climate Fund to help developing countries go low carbon
- To slow, halt and reverse the destruction of trees
- To set up ways to help developing countries access low-carbon technologies

DID YOU KNOW?

If global temperatures rise by even two degrees Celsius it would mean that 20%-30% of species could face extinction.

Source: Met Office

What you can do about climate change

Some further changes to the Earth's climate are inevitable, but there is still time to have a positive influence on the future. You can help minimise further changes and adapt to those that will happen through your decisions and actions. Read about simple things you can do to make a difference in 'Greener living: a quick guide to what you can do', which can be found on the Directgov website (www.direct.gov.uk).

> *"There is a greater than 90 per cent chance that global warming over the last 50 years is due to human activity. At the 2007 UN climate change conference in Bali, the world's nations agreed to negotiate on a deal to tackle climate change."*

www.direct.gov.uk

Mini glossary

static – *standing still*

greenhouse gases – *any gas which contributes to the greenhouse effect (an overall increase in the Earth's temperature). These include methane, carbon monoxide and carbon dioxide*

low-carbon technologies – *technology that is designed to release low levels of carbon dioxide in order to minimise pollution and climate change*

The marine environment

INFORMATION FROM Defra.

Our seas offer millions of people a chance to enjoy the natural environment; provide healthy, secure food supplies and other resources; and support employment in coastal communities. Healthy, productive, sustainable marine ecosystems contain rich and varied wildlife, plants and geological features. They provide a wide range of ecosystem services, including helping to mitigate the effects of climate change.

We subject our seas to competing demands, as well as pollution and other damage. They help to regulate our climate, but their ecosystems are threatened by warming and acidification. Some fish stocks are not fished at sustainable levels and some habitats and species are threatened by the pressures on our seas.

Marine issues are of global concern and the UK is taking a lead on issues such as ocean acidification. We are also taking a lead to protect whales and prevent illegal fishing.

Our seas are a common public resource so the Government aims to ensure they are sustainably managed for a range of social, environmental and economic benefits. The UK has national, EU and international marine conservation commitments. Defra decides upon marine protected areas, which play a key part in achieving biodiversity benefits. We are also tackling the issues of how best to strike a balance between conservation and development of marine resources. Supplies of fish as a healthy food source need to be secured, without destroying fish stocks and damaging the marine environment.

Key facts and figures

- Seas and oceans absorb 25% of global carbon emissions from human activity.
- UK seas contain rich and varied wildlife, with over 8,000 species represented.
- Seas provide revenue from oil and gas (£37 billion), maritime transport (£4.7 billion), leisure and recreation (£1.3 billion), coastal tourism (£5.3 billion), naval defence (£470 million), and fisheries and aquaculture (£400 million).
- Wind and tidal energy are likely to meet 50% of the UK's renewable energy needs.

The current situation and background

The Government's marine programme covers six areas:

1 Implementing the Marine Strategy Framework Directive

Defra is putting in place the Marine Strategy Framework Directive to secure good environmental status in our seas. This Directive requires EU member states to put in place measures to achieve or maintain good environmental status in their seas by 2020. The Government is turning the Directive's requirements into national legislation and deciding what good environmental status will mean for our seas, balancing our environmental ambitions against impacts on industry and society as a whole.

DID YOU KNOW?

In 1986 the International Whaling Commission banned commercial whaling (killing whales and selling their parts for profit), although Japan, Iceland and Norway continue the practice.

The marine environment

2 Managing our marine resources to secure sustainable development in our seas

New marine plans will be rolled out from 2011 to provide more strategic national and local decision-making to assist sustained economic growth and environmental protection. The Marine Management Organisation brings together management of a number of marine activities, including fishing, nature conservation, licensing and enforcement, and will also be responsible for the marine planning system.

3 Protecting, conserving and enhancing marine biodiversity

Defra is seeking to stop the decline in biodiversity, and allow recovery where appropriate. Marine protected areas are one of the major tools to conserve biodiversity in the marine environment. We are giving high priority to maintaining the International Whaling Commission's ban on commercial whaling.

DID YOU KNOW?

Seas provide revenue from oil and gas (£37 billion), maritime transport (£4.7 billion), leisure and recreation (£1.3 billion), coastal tourism (£5.3 billion), naval defence (£470 million) and fisheries and aquaculture (£400 million)

How serious is the decline and possible extinction of animal species, flora and fauna, natural habitats and ecosystems in your country?

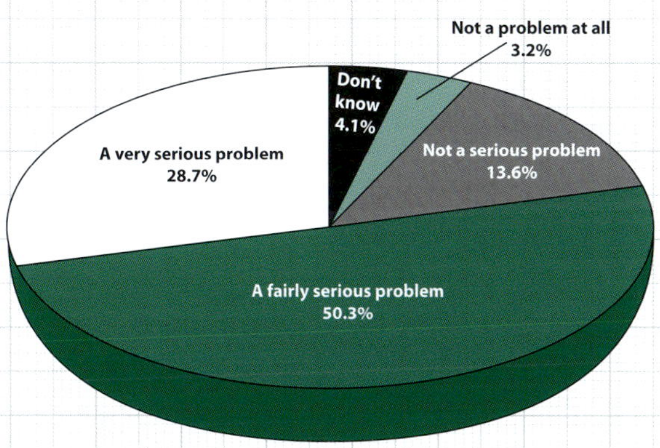

Source: Attitudes of Europeans towards the issue of biodiversity, © *European Commission*

4 Securing economically and environmentally sustainable fisheries

We are seeking new ways of managing fisheries at national, European and international levels. We want to secure long-term sustainable fisheries, support a viable fishing industry and provide secure, healthy food supplies.

5 Managing fish and seafood supply chain to provide secure, healthy food

We are looking for sustainable use and production throughout the fish supply chain. We are contributing to the Defra Food Strategy and Action Plan and taking forward the evidence from the Fish and Shellfish Roadmap to feed into fisheries reform. We are assessing the potential for increasing domestic shellfish and aquaculture production and we are also supporting a sustainable global fisheries trade, including controls on illegal, unreported and unregulated fishing.

6 Understanding and adapting to the changing marine environment

As we face serious challenges, such as climate change, ocean acidification and depletion of some fish stocks, high-quality marine science is essential. We are working with European partners to assess the impacts of climate change on our seas and ways we can adapt to this.

Information from Defra. © Crown copyright

www.defra.gov.uk

Mini glossary

mitigate *– make less severe*

acidification *– the process whereby something becomes more acidic*

directive *– an order or instruction*

reform *– putting in place changes to make things better*

depletion *– using something up; making something less*

Floods and droughts

INFORMATION FROM THE Global Water Partnership.

Floods are the most common natural disaster and cause more deaths and damage than any other type. Yet floods also sustain aquatic life and riverine biodiversity, recharge aquifers, enrich soils and, in some of the world's poorest areas, provide an important means of irrigation.

Affects the already vulnerable

One of the most severe by-products of global warming and climate change is widespread drought, which will affect a large number of nations in the future, especially those in regions already prone to experiencing them. Droughts have a major impact on food security, especially for vulnerable populations, and can also have major long-term socio-economic impacts. Countries reliant on hydropower for electricity generation experience power shortages. Countries reliant upon rain-fed agriculture can find that the GDP for the country as a whole is significantly reduced in times of drought.

> ***"Floods are the most common natural disaster and cause more deaths and damage than any other type."***

Building resilience

The challenge is to reduce the negative impact of floods and droughts on human lives and livelihoods by reducing the risk of such disasters, and by building resilience of people and communities. Prediction and monitoring are key to developing early warning systems and preparing for disaster situations. Approaches should be holistic, taking into account the needs of communities, the built environment and aquatic ecosystems within the area where they occur. Hence water-related disaster management needs to be integrated with other planning, and also address the fact that many poor people live in high-risk locations.

www.gwp.org

Mini glossary

- ***aquatic*** – *water-based*
- ***riverine*** – *related to a river*
- ***irrigation*** – *supplying water for dry land*
- ***socio-economic*** – *a combination of social and economical factors*
- ***hydropower*** – *water-powered*
- ***GDP*** – *gross domestic product – how much money a country makes from its goods and services*
- ***holistic*** – *dealing with all aspects*

Population and the environment

WHERE WE'RE HEADED and what we can do.

Many environmental problems will be easier to address if world population peaks at eight billion rather than continuing to grow to 11 billion or higher. The good news: there is already a global consensus on how to slow population growth, with programmes that improve human wellbeing at very little cost.

World population is still growing

While the rate of population growth has slowed in most parts of the world, overall growth continues. We increase by nearly 80 million people every year – this is the same as adding another US to the world every four years. The number of people on the planet has doubled since 1960 and will reach seven billion in 2011.

Tomorrow's population size will be determined today

We often hear the prediction that world population will reach nine billion in 2050, but there are a range of possibilities – from eight billion to 11 billion. By 2100, the range is even wider – from six billion to 16 billion.

Tomorrow's population size depends on the choices couples make about having children today, but far too many lack the means to plan and space their pregnancies. Around the world, 215 million women want to prevent pregnancy but need contraception. In nations where access to contraception is limited – such as Yemen, Afghanistan and much of Sub-Saharan Africa – women continue to have an average of more than five children. And the need for contraception is growing. Nearly half the world's population is under the age of 25 and entering their childbearing years.

Eight billion would be better than 11 billion – for people and the planet

The impact of population growth on the environment is affected by consumption, technology, urbanisation and other factors. Still, slower population growth could reduce pressure on natural systems, and research shows that a host of environmental problems – including the growth of greenhouse gases, water scarcity and biodiversity loss – would be easier to address if world population peaked at eight billion, rather than continuing to 11 billion or more.

Climate change is expected to result in less agricultural production in many parts of the world, and will make limited water supplies even more difficult to manage. Slower population growth would help people adapt to climate change, reduce the scale of human vulnerability to these impacts, and give nations a chance to make important investments in healthcare, education and sustainable economic development.

Population and the environment

We know how to slow population growth

Half a century of experience has shown that the best way to slow growth is to make sure that people are able to make decisions about whether they have children, and when they have them. This means providing access to contraception and other reproductive health services. It means education and employment opportunities, especially for women. And it means tackling gender and economic inequities that are associated with rapid population growth.

There are success stories: international family planning programmes, supported by the US, have enabled women around the world to plan and space their pregnancies. Partly as a result of those programmes, contraceptive use in developing countries rose from less than ten per cent in the 1960s to 60 per cent today, and fertility rates fell from six children per woman to three. But with 215 million women around the world still in need of contraceptives, the job is not yet done.

“Tomorrow’s population size depends on the choices couples make about having children today.”

There is already a global agreement on population and development goals

We already have a UN agreement on population, endorsed by 179 developed and developing nations in 1994. Countries at that time agreed on a plan to slow population growth through universal access to reproductive health services, empowering girls and women, and combating poverty. These were reaffirmed in the UN Millennium Development Goals earlier this decade.

Family planning programmes are cost-effective and contribute to human wellbeing

Family planning programmes are relatively inexpensive. Meeting the demand for family planning in the developing world would require an additional $3.6 billion annually. The US share of the cost is about $1 billion. Meeting the need for family planning would help millions adapt to climate change, and prevent 53 million unplanned pregnancies, 150,000 maternal deaths and 25 million abortions.

“The world’s population increase by nearly 80 million people every year – this is the same as adding another US to the world every four years.”

But governments are not keeping their promises

Despite the low cost and many benefits of family planning programmes, the world’s nations have yet to provide sufficient resources to pay for them. While developing countries are spending about half of what they pledged in 1994, developed countries have provided less than a quarter of the promised funding.

Environmentalists have an important role to play

More voices are needed to demonstrate the broad base of support for these vital programmes that benefit human health and wellbeing, as well as the global environment.

Population and the environment

Simple points about population and the environment

Rapid population growth increases pressure on resources that are already over-used, including water, forests, land and the atmosphere. If current population growth rates continue, the world's population would grow from around seven billion today to 11 billion by 2050.

The rate of population growth in the future responds to actions we take today, including providing access to family planning.

More than 215 million women around the world want to avoid pregnancy but need contraception.

Family planning stands out as an opportunity to improve the health of women and children, while increasing people's resilience to environmental challenges.

Achieving universal access to family planning and reproductive health services will improve the health and wellbeing of women and families. Slowing population growth will also ease pressure on natural resources and improve prospects for solving environmental challenges.

Mini glossary

consensus – *general agreement*

inequity – *unfairness*

endorsed – *supported by*

universal – *for everyone*

environmentalist – *someone who works to protect the environment*

Information from Population Action International.

www.populationaction.org

Water statistics

STATISTICAL INFORMATION FROM WaterAid.

A global crisis

- 884 million people in the world do not have access to safe water. This is roughly one in eight of the world's population. (WHO/UNICEF)
- 2.6 billion people in the world do not have access to adequate sanitation. This is almost two-fifths of the world's population. (WHO/UNICEF)
- 1.4 million children die every year from diarrhoea caused by unclean water and poor sanitation – 4,000 child deaths a day or one child every 20 seconds. This equates to 160 infant school classrooms lost every single day to an entirely preventable public health crisis. (WHO/WaterAid)

What has WaterAid done?

- Since 1981, we have reached 15.89 million people with safe water.
- Since 2004, we have reached 11.02 million people with sanitation.
- In 2010/11 we reached 1.45 million people with safe water and 1.62 million people with sanitation.
- Just £15 can enable one person to access a lasting supply of safe water, improved hygiene and sanitation. (WaterAid)

Sanitation

- Diarrhoea kills more children every year than AIDS, malaria and measles combined. (WHO)
- Children living in households with no toilet are twice as likely to get diarrhoea as those with a toilet. (WEDC)
- Every year, around 60 million children in the developing world are born into households without access to sanitation. (UN Water)
- One gram of human faeces can contain 10,000,000 viruses, 1,000,000 bacteria, 1,000 parasite cysts, 100 parasite eggs. (UNICEF)
- At any given time, close to half the people in the developing world are suffering from one or more of the main diseases associated with dirty water and inadequate sanitation, such as diarrhoea, guinea worm, trachoma and schistosomiasis. (UNDP Human Development Report 2006)
- Half the hospital beds in developing countries are filled with people suffering from diseases associated with poor water, sanitation and hygiene. (UNDP Human Development Report 2006)

Water statistics

Hygiene

- Hand-washing with soap at critical times can reduce the incidence of diarrhoea by up to 47%. (UN Water)
- The integrated approach of providing water, sanitation and hygiene reduces the number of deaths caused by diarrhoeal diseases by an average of 65%. (WHO)

Education and livelihoods

- For every $1 invested in water and sanitation, on average $8 is returned in increased productivity. (UNDP)
- Lack of safe water and sanitation costs Sub-Saharan Africa around 5% of its Gross Domestic Product (GDP) each year. (UNDP)

Water

- The weight of water that women in Africa and Asia carry on their heads is commonly 20kg, the same as the average UK airport luggage allowance. (HDR)
- The average person in the developing world uses ten litres of water every day for their drinking, washing and cooking. (WSSCC)
- The average European uses 200 litres of water every day for their drinking, washing and cooking. North Americans use 400 litres. (HDR)
- On current trends, over the next 20 years humans will use 40% more water than they do now. (UNEP)
- Agriculture accounts for over 80% of the world's water consumption. (UNEP)
- 97.5% of the Earth's water is saltwater. If the world's water fitted into a bucket, only one teaspoonful would be drinkable. (HDR

Water statistics

Millennium Development Goals

- The world is on track to meet or even exceed the MDG for safe drinking water – to halve the proportion of people without access to safe water by 2015. However, even though we are on track globally, 884 million people are still without access. (WHO/UNICEF)
- The world is seriously off track to meet the sanitation MDG target – to halve the proportion of people without access to sanitation by 2015. If current rates of progress continue, the global sanitation goal will be met 30 years too late. In Sub-Saharan Africa, the sanitation target in that region is not due to be met for another 200 years. (WHO/UNICEF)
- Nearly half the people who gained access to water between 1990 and 2008 live in India and China. (WHO/UNICEF)

Financing the sector

- Over the past ten years, aid to health and HIV/AIDS in Sub-Saharan Africa has increased by nearly 500%, while aid to water and sanitation has increased by only 79%. (OECD)

Water and sanitation in history

- South Korea made huge investments in water and sanitation during the 1960s, when its per capita income was the same as Ghana's, and during that decade, under-five mortality more than halved, while the number of medical staff stayed virtually the same. (WaterAid)
- In the UK, the expansion of water and sanitation infrastructure in the 1880s contributed to a 15-year increase in life expectancy in the following four decades. (HDR, 2006)

DID YOU KNOW?

- In the UK, each person uses on average 150 litres of water daily.
- The average household uses over 100,000 litres of water every year.
- Imagine 317 pints of milk and that's 150 litres of water.
- One-fifth of a household's carbon footprint comes just from heating water for baths, showers and washing up.

Information from WaterAid.

www.wateraid.org

Mini glossary

sanitation – *the disposal of sewage and effluence; keeping clean and germ-free*

Sub-Saharan Africa – *the area that lies south of the Sahara desert in Africa*

Forgotten forests have vital role in keeping deserts at bay

INFORMATION FROM THE CHARTERED Institution of Water and Environmental Management (CIWEM).

Dryland forests are at the forefront of the battle to halt the spread of deserts in arid countries, maintaining the productivity of farmland and a sustainable way of life. They cover a fifth of the land area of arid zones, yet few people have heard of them, and fewer appreciate their value. That must change, says the Chartered Institution of Water and Environmental Management (CIWEM) on World Day to Combat Desertification.

Deforestation conjures up images of areas of tropical rainforest the size of small European counties or US states being cleared by commercial logging or ranching interests, or perhaps to make space for biofuel crop plantations. But in countries of the world where populations face extreme poverty because of poor crop yield or failure, made worse by encroaching deserts, healthy forests are a lifeline.

In such arid and semi-arid zones, poverty and need for food and fuel can lead to dryland forests being cleared for farmland as well as for wood fuel to burn. Often these parts of the world face the greatest pressures from development and population growth.

This forest loss leads to less food availability for browsing livestock as well as to loss of biodiversity. But the effect can be reversed and good farming practice and maintenance or replanting of forests can have dramatic and positive effects for farmers, providing shelter for crops, food for livestock, a sustainable supply of fuel and far fewer failed crop sowings.

CIWEM's Executive Director, Nick Reeves, says:

"Without wishing to sound crass, dryland forests aren't glam. They don't have the soaring majesty of many tropical and some temperate forests, or the abundant biodiversity that rainforests support, but they are of vital importance to developing countries, particularly through the support systems they provide.

Their benefits are often very immediately felt, but somehow they have been below the radar of the international community. There is a real need to spread good land management practices in dryland areas and to sell the benefits to communities of maintaining and improving their forests. It is important that the international community support these measures."

Information from CIWEM. © CIWEM

www.ciwem.org.uk

Mini glossary

dryland forest – *forests that grow in areas of low rainfall*

deforestation – *clearing trees*

arid – *having little or no rainfall*

Activities

Brainstorm

Brainstorm to find out what you know about protecting the environment.

1. What causes climate change and what effect does it have on the environment?

....

....

....

2. What is being done to combat it?

....

....

....

Oral activities

3. We know that many environmental problems could be solved if the world's population stopped growing. Prepare a presentation explaining different ways to slow down population growth.

NOTES..........

....

....

4. Many people in developing countries have to walk long distances to fetch or carry water. In groups, discuss how you might design a water-transportation device. The device would need to be easy to carry, lightweight and waterproof. Note down the materials you would use and how your device would work, and then compare your idea with other groups.

NOTES..........

....

Moral dilemma

5. Read the article on page 25. Imagine that you are building a new hotel complex in an area that has a large patch of dryland forest. The forest is not diverse enough to allow wildlife tours, and it is not very attractive. It feels like a waste of land. Someone suggests that you take down the forest, use the trees for fuel, and donate some of the land to the local community to use as farmland. However, you are aware that maintaining the forest could have even more positive effects for local farmers. Is there a solution? What do you do? Discuss your thoughts with a partner.

Activities

Research activities

6. Read *A history of climate change* on pages 14 and 15. Research the effects of climate change, for example extreme weather events and rising sea levels. Are there any events in recent history that could be attributed to climate change? Create a timeline of these events.

CONCLUSION ....

....

....

7. Research the global population and find out how much it has grown over the last five years. Use your findings to create a line graph. Next, investigate the current population of at least ten different countries, and use your information to create a bar graph.

NOTES ....

....

....

Written activities

Complete the following activities in your exercise books or on a sheet of paper.

8. Write an article for your local newspaper explaining why the marine environment is important and what we need to do to conserve it.

9. Watch the 2004 film *The Day After Tomorrow* and write a review, discussing how the film portrays climate change.

10. Write a short story set in Britain 100 years in the future. What changes has climate change had on our environment? What impact would changes brought about as a result of global warming have on our day-to-day lives?

Design activities

12. Imagine you have been asked to create a new website which will explain climate change to young children. The website will need to explain what climate change is, its causes, effects and what is being done to tackle it. On paper, design the home page for the website, and two other pages of your choice (for example, the 'Effects of Climate Change' page and an 'Activities' page).

13. Create an A3 poster highlighting key facts about how we use water around the world, and the issues surrounding water use.

Key Facts

- *Around 1.6 million people die from exposure to cooking stove smoke inside their homes. About half of these deaths occur in India and China. Most victims are children and women from poor rural families who lack access to safe water, sanitation and modern household fuels. (page 1)*
- *One million people die from malaria, mostly in Sub-Saharan African countries. (page 1)*
- *Green infrastructure can help to balance the effects of climate change by managing temperature, water resources, surface water, flooding and habitat networks. (page 3)*
- *Over the past 30 years Europe has made a lot of progress in tackling environmental problems caused by harmful substances, such as air pollutants, sewage and hazardous waste. But environmental problems related to European production and consumption are getting worse. (page 5)*
- *Paper, glass, plastic bottles, garden waste, fridges, shoes, batteries – all of these and more can be recycled, helping to save energy and new materials. (page 7)*
- *Around 40% of waste from households is currently recycled, as of 2011, compared to 11% in 2000/01. (page 11)*
- *55% of municipal waste generated in the UK is sent to landfill, compared to an EU-27 average of 40%. (page 11)*
- *In 2007, the IPCC announced that the planet has warmed about 0.75 degrees Celsius since the beginning of the 20th century. It said there is a greater than 90 per cent chance that global warming over the last 50 years is due to human activity. (page 15)*
- *Seas and oceans absorb 25% of global carbon emissions from human activity. (page 16)*
- *UK seas contain rich and varied wildlife, with over 8,000 species represented. (page 16)*
- *One of the most severe by-products of global warming and climate change is widespread drought, which will affect a large number of nations in the future, especially those in regions already prone to experiencing them. (page 18)*
- *We increase by nearly 80 million people every year – this is the same as adding another US to the world every four years. (page 19)*
- *The number of people on the planet has doubled since 1960 and will reach seven billion in 2011. (page 19)*
- *More than 215 million women around the world want to avoid pregnancy but need contraception. (page 21)*

Glossary

Biodiversity – *The number and variety of organisms found in a specific area. A balanced, healthy ecosystem will support a large number of species, making it rich in biodiversity. Human impact on the environment (for example, through pollution or cutting down trees) can reduce biodiversity.*

Climate change – *Climate change describes a global change in the balance of energy absorbed into the atmosphere. This imbalance can be caused by natural or human processes. It can cause either regional or global changes in weather averages and the frequency of natural disasters such as floods and earthquakes.*

Ecosystem – *A natural system where living things interact with each other to create and preserve an environment which can sustain them.*

Environment – *The complex physical, geographic, biological, social, cultural and political conditions that surround an organism, affecting its form and the nature of its survival.*

E-waste – *E-waste stands for electronic waste. It is made up of everyday electrical goods such as mobile phones, televisions, stereos, PCs and printers. European Union regulations require it to be properly recycled, either here or in other developed countries.*

Global warming – *This refers to a rise in global average temperatures, caused by higher levels of greenhouse gases entering the atmosphere. Global warming is affecting the Earth in a number of ways, including melting the polar ice caps, which is leading to rising sea levels.*

Infrastructure – *The systems and services which support a community or society, such as transport, power and communication systems, as well as public institutions such as schools.*

Kyoto Protocol – *In 1997, the Kyoto Protocol was agreed. Kyoto was the first international treaty to set legally binding emissions cuts for industrialised nations. It was signed by 178 countries and came into force in 2005.*

Landfill – *A type of waste disposal in which solid waste is buried underground, between layers of dirt. Biodegradable products will eventually break down and be absorbed into the soil: however, non-biodegradable products such as plastic carrier bags will not break down (or will do so very, very slowly).*

Pollution – *Toxic substances which are released into the environment: for example, harmful gases or chemicals.*

Recycling – *Converting waste into new products and materials: this reduces the use of raw materials. For example, waste office paper can be recycled by pulping and processing it to make new paper.*

Sanitation – *Sanitation is the disposal of human sewage. Poor sanitation can lead to disease and polluted drinking water.*

Sustainability – *Sustainability means living within the limits of the planet's resources so they do not run out and are preserved for future generations. Sustainable living should maintain a balanced and healthy environment.*

Water scarcity – *A lack of access to fresh drinking water. This is often a big problem for communities in regions with very dry climates, such as Sub-Saharan Africa.*